Seasonal Soups

Seasonal Soups

First published in 2014 as Fraser's Seasonal Soups by Kitchen Press Ltd
1 Windsor Place
Dundee
DD2 1BG

2nd edition, Seasonal Soups, published in 2018

This edition published in 2022

Text © Fraser Reid 2022

Illustrations © Jen Collins 2022

Photography by Clair Irwin

Cover design by Sam Paton

Designed by Andrew Forteath

All rights reserved. No part of this publication may be reproduced, stored in a retrieval system, or transmitted in any format or by any means, electronic, mechanical, photocopying or otherwise, without prior permission of the copyright owners.

A CIP catalogue record for this book is available from the British Library

ISBN: 9781916316577

Printed by GPS Group in Bosnia and Herzegovina

10	**January**
22	**February**
32	**March**
44	**April**
54	**May**
64	**June**
74	**July**
84	**August**
94	**September**
106	**October**
116	**November**
126	**December**
138	Index

Who would have thought the nostalgic taste of a pea pod could create a cookbook. My journey as a greengrocer started in the summer of 2009 when I came across a thriving village shop in Northern Ireland packed with local, seasonal produce.

The owner gave us some of their fresh peas to try, something I hadn't eaten since I was a kid, and I started to think – where could I find a shop like this in my home town of Dundee? Incredibly, at that point, there were no dedicated greengrocers shops in the whole city, so I decided it was time to open one. Three months later Fraser's Fruit & Veg opened its doors.

Our premise was to provide our customers with as much fresh and local produce as we could get. Dundee is incredibly lucky to be surrounded by great farming lands with a massive variety of fresh produce and we even buy produce from local allotments and gardens. That's the key really: to get produce harvested that morning and onto the shelves within the next couple of hours. It was the thrill of seeing this ever-changing harvest that inspired us to make soup bags. We wanted to make it easier for our customers to cook at home and try out new flavours and ingredients.

Introd

Our first soup bag was a very simple Lentil, and as the weeks and years went by our recipes became more creative, elaborate and damn tasty. I like to experiment and try out new flavours; I'm constantly thinking – could that meal I just ate be turned into a soup? It's great fun and we try and keep our recipes as simple as possible so people don't have to go searching for obscure ingredients. The soup bags were a hit from day one, and even more fulfilling than seeing a new generation of novice cooks buying them was seeing people who have been making soup for 50 years trying them out.

We had one customer who had been married for 57 years and had never cooked for his wife but every Tuesday he would come in and buy a soup bag and cook it for her. Soup is simple!

We hope you enjoy making these soups as much as we've enjoyed creating them.

Fraser

I hate to say it, but I think it's almost completely pointless making your own vegetable stock – essentially, a soup – to make vegetable soup. I always use good quality vegetable stock cubes, crumbled into the pan along with boiling water to save on washing up – though if you prefer to make up the stock before pouring it in, go right ahead. If you're not a vegetarian and you have some home-made chicken stock, use the same amounts as specified of boiling water; it will always add a lovely depth of flavour.

A Word About Stocks

You would think that January is a drab and cold month where everyone is trying to get back into a healthy routine after the excesses of Christmas and Hogmanay, but let me tell you, it's amazing for a fruit and veg shop. Everyone is trying to get their five-a-day, and what better way to do this than by having soup for lunch or dinner?

January also has some amazing ingredients bang in season. Citrus fruit is as good as it gets with Seville oranges and the sweetest clementines. In the veg world, there's nothing better than some turnip on Burns Night or using super sweet carrots and parsnips and balancing them with spices and fruits in soups and casseroles.

Sweet Potato, Tomato & Roasted Garlic Soup

An absolute crowd pleaser which children will love too. The roasted garlic gives the soup an incredible depth and sweetness.

Serves 4

1 garlic bulb
1 tablespoon olive oil or butter
1 onion, peeled and diced
1 carrot, peeled and diced
3 tomatoes, roughly chopped
1 large sweet potato, peeled and roughly chopped
1 stock cube
salt and freshly ground black pepper

Preheat the oven to 190°C. Pop the whole garlic bulb on a baking tray, drizzle with a little oil and bake in the oven for 30 minutes.

Meanwhile, heat the oil or butter in a pot and fry the onion and carrots on a low heat for 5–10 minutes.

Add the tomatoes and sweet potato and give everything a stir.

Pour in 1.2 litres of boiling water and crumble in the stock cube. Bring to the boil, and then turn the heat to low and simmer for 20 minutes.

Remove the garlic from the oven and squeeze the soft, sweet cloves out of their skin and into the soup. Blend everything 'til smooth and season to taste with salt and plenty of freshly ground black pepper.

Souper Noodle Broth

No apologies for the pun! This one's a pile of healthy greens, chillies and ginger that's great for you and great tasting too.

Serves 4

1 tablespoon sunflower oil
1 thumb-sized piece of ginger, peeled and very finely chopped
2 large garlic cloves, peeled and very finely chopped
1 red chilli, very finely chopped
1 carrot, peeled and very finely chopped
2 stock cubes
1 head of pak choi, sliced
1 or 2 leaves of cavolo nero or kale, very finely sliced
1 nest of egg or rice noodles
1 spring onion, roughly chopped

Heat the sunflower oil in a pot, then add the ginger, garlic, chilli and carrot. Fry on a low heat for 5–10 minutes until they're soft and smell good.

Pour in 1.6 litres of boiling water, then crumble in the stock cubes and add the pak choi, kale and noodles. Turn up the heat and bring everything to the boil.

Lower the heat and simmer for 5 minutes until the noodles are cooked, then garnish with the spring onion.

Feel free to add a couple of dashes of soy sauce and pepper before serving.

Persian Root & Fruit

This is the kind of flavour that I love: the sweetness from the root veg and pear balances well with the aromatic spices. This spice mix is great with any root veg soup.

Serves 4

1 tablespoon olive oil or butter
1 onion, peeled and roughly chopped
2 garlic cloves, peeled and finely chopped
1 teaspoon paprika
1 teaspoon coriander seeds
1 teaspoon cumin seeds
2 carrots, peeled and roughly chopped
1 parsnip, peeled and roughly chopped
300g turnip, peeled and roughly chopped
1 pear, peeled, cored and roughly chopped
2 stock cubes
salt and freshly ground black pepper

Heat a pot on a medium-low heat and add the oil or butter. Fry the onion and garlic for 5–10 minutes until they are soft.

Toast the paprika, coriander and cumin seeds in a dry frying pan over a medium heat for a minute or two – they are ready when they start to release their smell.

Add the spices to the softened onion and garlic, and then stir in the carrots, parsnip, turnip and pear and give everything a mix.

Pour in 1.2 litres of boiling water and crumble in the stock cubes. Bring everything to the boil. Reduce the heat and simmer for 25 minutes.

Season the soup well to taste and blitz until completely smooth.

Golden Cauliflower & Almond

The Spanish love to use cauliflower and almond together, and giving it a twist of golden turmeric and carrot turns this soup into something altogether different and incredibly tasty.

Serves 4

1 tablespoon olive oil or butter
1 onion, peeled and finely chopped
2 medium carrots, peeled and roughly chopped
2 garlic cloves, peeled and finely chopped
60g ground almonds
1 cauliflower, leaves removed, roughly chopped
1 teaspoon ground turmeric
2 stock cubes
salt and freshly ground black pepper

Heat a pot on a medium-low heat and add the oil or butter. When it's hot, add the onion, carrots and garlic and fry for 5–10 minutes until they soften slightly.

Put in the ground almonds, cauliflower and turmeric and give everything a stir.

Pour in 1.2 litres of boiling water, then crumble the stock cubes into the pot and bring everything to the boil. Turn down the heat and simmer it for 20 minutes.

Blend the soup until smooth and season to taste with salt and freshly ground black pepper.

Rabbie Burns

We had fun with this play on words, and the soup makes a nice starter on Burns Night. The pepper adds a touch of sweetness but is mostly there to add colour: soup tastes nicer when it's not beige! For a milder flavour, deseed the chilli before you chop it.

Serves 4

1 tablespoon olive oil or butter
1 onion, peeled and roughly chopped
1 chilli, finely chopped
1 red pepper, deseeded and roughly chopped
750g turnip, peeled and roughly chopped
2 stock cubes
salt and freshly ground black pepper

Heat a pot on a medium-low heat and add the tablespoon of oil or butter. Fry the onions, chilli and red pepper for 5–10 minutes, until everything is soft but not browned.

Stir in the turnip, and then add the stock cubes dissolved in 1.2 litres of boiling water.

Bring everything to the boil and then simmer for 30 minutes until the turnip is absolutely tender.

Blend the soup until smooth and season with salt and plenty of freshly ground black pepper. Garnish with a little more finely chopped red chilli if you like it spicy.

February, the shortest month of the year, is the gateway to spring. It can either feel like the depths of winter or you can start to look forward to better days. It's a little bit of an in between month for fruit and veg too, but Sicilian blood oranges – which I love – hit the shelves in Feb and the shop is full of local root veg, Brussels sprouts and cabbages.

Spanish Split Pea

This soup was inspired by the classic pea and ham but as usual we gave it a little twist. I started out making a soup with chorizo and split pea (very nice if you feel like trying it out) but decided to make it vegetarian by adding extra garlic, some smoked paprika and celery for a little more peppery depth. This is an easy one to make out of store cupboard ingredients, a bit of limp celery from the bottom of the fridge and a spare onion. The split peas do not need to be soaked beforehand.

Serves 4

1 tablespoon olive oil or butter
1 onion, peeled and diced
1 celery stick, diced
1 carrot, peeled and diced
2 garlic cloves, peeled and finely chopped
350g split peas, rinsed
1 teaspoon smoked paprika
1 stock cube
salt and freshly ground black pepper

Put the oil or butter in a pot over a medium-low heat, then add the onion, celery, carrot and garlic and fry gently for 5–10 minutes until they are soft.

Add the split peas and smoked paprika and give everything a stir.

Pour in 2 litres of boiling water, crumble in the stock cube and then turn up the heat and boil hard for 5 minutes. Reduce the heat, cover and simmer for 45–50 minutes, keeping a close eye on it for the last 10 minutes to make sure it doesn't get too thick (if it does, add a splash of boiling water).

Blend the soup 'til smooth and season with salt and freshly ground black pepper.

Leek, Potato & Roasted Garlic

Our take on the classic soup – it's astounding that four ingredients can create such a wonderful and comforting soup.

Serves 4

1 garlic bulb, unpeeled
1 tablespoon olive oil or butter
1 large leek, washed and finely sliced
500g potatoes, peeled and diced into 2cm cubes
2 stock cubes
salt and freshly ground black pepper

Preheat your oven to 190°C. Put the whole garlic bulb on a baking tray and bake for 30 minutes.

Meanwhile, heat the oil or butter in a pot and fry the leek on a low heat for 5–10 minutes.

Add the potatoes and give everything a stir.

Pour in 1.2 litres of boiling water and crumble in the stock cubes. Bring to the boil, and then turn the heat to low and simmer for 20 minutes.

When the garlic is done, squeeze the soft, sweet cloves out of their skin and add them to the soup. Blend everything 'til smooth and season to taste with salt and freshly ground black pepper.

Sweet Potato, Lentil & Blood Orange

This is a lovely sweet and zesty soup: it can be made with ordinary oranges but it's a great excuse to use sweet Sicilian blood oranges which are in the shops from December to March.

Serves 4

1 tablespoon olive oil or butter
1 onion, peeled and roughly chopped
2 garlic cloves, peeled and finely chopped
1 small sweet potato, peeled and roughly chopped
1 carrot, peeled and roughly chopped
175g red lentils, rinsed well
2 stock cubes
juice and zest of 1 blood orange
salt and freshly ground black pepper

Put a pot on a medium-low heat and add the oil or butter. When it's hot, fry the onion and garlic for 5–10 minutes until they're soft.

Add the sweet potato, carrot and lentils and give everything a stir.

Pour in 1.2 litres of boiling water, and crumble in the stock cubes along with the juice and zest of the orange. Bring everything to the boil, and then turn down the heat and simmer for 20 minutes.

Season the soup to taste with salt and freshly ground black pepper and blend until smooth.

Curried Parsnip

Everyone loves curried parsnip soup; it's so simple to make and so tasty. It's really easy to vary too: just change up the spices – any mix of mild and aromatic spices like cumin, coriander, turmeric and paprika work well. Sometimes I add a teaspoon of honey to help bring out the natural sweetness of the parsnips.

Serves 4

1 tablespoon olive oil or butter
1 onion, peeled and diced
2 garlic cloves, peeled and finely chopped
1 teaspoon mild curry powder
½ teaspoon ground ginger
750g parsnips, peeled and roughly chopped
2 stock cubes
salt and freshly ground black pepper

Heat the oil or butter in a pot, then add the onions and garlic and fry everything on a medium-low heat for 5–10 minutes.

Meanwhile, put the spices into a dry frying pan over a medium heat and toast them until they start to release their fragrance (about 2–3 minutes).

Add the toasted spices and the chopped parsnips to the softened onions and give everything a mix.

Pour in 1.2 litres of boiling water, crumble in the stock cubes and bring it all to the boil.

Reduce the heat and simmer for 20–25 minutes.

Blend the soup until smooth and season with salt and plenty of freshly ground black pepper.

We hate March in the shop – it's a little bit too late for the winter veg and the spring and summer stuff is just being planted in the ground. We are desperate to see the start of the spring produce so have to be creative with our soup ingredients and head to the store cupboard to keep things exciting.

Alternative Scotch Broth

This is a nice introduction to the ugly root vegetable celeriac. It has a peppery taste and a creamy texture and balances really well with woody herbs. In this soup we use it with carrots, leeks and barley, but feel free to use any mixture of different root vegetables.

Serves 4

1 tablespoon olive oil or butter
1 medium leek, washed and finely chopped
2 carrots, peeled and diced
½ celeriac, trimmed and diced
100g pearl barley, rinsed
2 stock cubes
salt and freshly ground black pepper

Heat a pot on a medium heat and add the oil or butter. Fry the leek for 5–10 minutes, until it's soft but not coloured.

Add the carrot, celeriac and barley to the pot and continue to fry for 2 minutes, giving everything a mix while you go.

Pour in 1.5 litres of boiling water, crumble in the stock cubes then bring everything to the boil. Turn down the heat and simmer gently for 25 minutes.

Season the soup well to taste – lots of freshly ground black pepper is good here.

Chilli Pepper Chickpea

Try saying that quickly three times! A great warming but fresh soup; you can eat it chunky, but if you blend it then you will really taste the nutty flavour of the chickpeas.

Serves 4

- 1 tablespoon olive oil or butter
- 1 red onion, peeled and roughly chopped
- 2 garlic cloves, peeled and finely chopped
- 1 chilli, deseeded (optional) and finely chopped
- 3 carrots, peeled and roughly chopped
- 1 red pepper, deseeded and roughly chopped
- 1 × 400g tin chickpeas, drained
- 2 stock cubes
- salt and freshly ground black pepper

Heat a pot on a medium heat and add the oil or butter. Fry the onion, garlic, chilli, carrots and red pepper for 10 minutes until soft but not coloured.

Stir in the drained chickpeas, give it all a good mix, and then add 1.2 litres of boiling water and the crumbled stock cubes. Bring to the boil and then lower the heat and simmer for 20 minutes.

Season the soup to taste and either serve as it is or put in the blender and blitz until smooth.

Granny Smith Green

Named after the famous bright green apple, this soup oozes healthiness and is a fantastic blend of leafy greens, silky smooth courgettes and cashew. This soup could be changed really easily by substituting basil or parsley for the coriander.

Serves 4

1 tablespoon olive oil or butter
1 onion, peeled and roughly chopped
2 garlic cloves, peeled and finely chopped
1 large carrot, peeled and roughly chopped
1 large courgette, roughly chopped
50g unsalted cashew nuts
1 bunch fresh coriander, finely chopped
2 stock cubes
250g washed spinach
salt and freshly ground black pepper

Heat the olive oil or butter in a pot over a medium-low heat. Fry the onion and garlic for 5–10 minutes until they soften slightly.

Add the carrot, courgette, cashews and fresh coriander to the pot, mixing everything together.

Pour in a litre of boiling water, crumble in the stock cubes and bring it all to the boil. Turn down the heat and simmer for 20 minutes.

Take the pot off the heat and stir in the spinach until it wilts.

Blend the soup for at least 3 minutes to get a really silky smooth finish. Season it to taste and, if you like, add a drizzle of olive oil.

Smokey Sweet Potato & Butterbean

Hands down this is one of my favourite soup recipes. The creamy butterbeans are the perfect balance for the smoky paprika and sweetness of the potatoes.

Serves 4

- 1 tablespoon olive oil or butter
- 1 onion, peeled and roughly chopped
- 2 garlic cloves, peeled and finely chopped
- 1 sweet potato, peeled and roughly chopped
- 1 or 2 carrots, peeled and roughly chopped
- 1 × 400g tin butterbeans, drained
- 1 teaspoon smoked paprika
- 2 stock cubes
- salt and freshly ground black pepper

Heat a pot on a medium heat and add the oil or butter. Fry the onion and garlic for 5–10 minutes until they soften slightly.

Add the sweet potato, carrots, drained butter beans and smoked paprika to the pot, and stir to mix everything together.

Pour in 1.2 litres of boiling water, crumble in the stock cubes, and then bring it all to the boil. Turn down the heat and simmer for 20 minutes.

Blend the soup and season to taste with salt, black pepper and a pinch or two of smoked paprika.

Spicy (Or Not) Tomato & Lentil

The chilli is optional here – the soup is great either way. If you do want some heat, why not try a Kashmiri or chipotle chilli to vary the flavour.

Serves 4

- 1 tablespoon olive oil
- 1 onion, peeled and roughly chopped
- 2 garlic cloves, peeled and finely chopped
- 1 × 400g tin tomatoes
- 2cm fresh ginger, peeled and finely chopped
- 1 teaspoon ground cumin
- 1 chilli, deseeded (optional) and finely chopped
- 175g red lentils, rinsed
- 1 stock cube
- salt and freshly ground black pepper

Heat the olive oil or butter in a pot on a medium-low heat. Fry the onion and garlic for 5–10 minutes until they are soft.

Add the tomatoes, ginger, ground cumin, half of the chilli and the lentils and give everything a stir.

Pour in 1.2 litres of boiling water, crumble in the stock cube and bring everything to the boil. Turn down the heat and simmer for 30 minutes.

Blend the soup and season well. Add a little more chopped chilli to each bowl according to taste.

This is the start of the new season produce coming in: some early British asparagus, spinach and look out for the slim pink stems of Yorkshire rhubarb. This rhubarb, although fairly pricey, is the sign that the warmer temperatures are on their way. Its tender and tangy flavour will help lift a rich dessert but I've not made it work in soup – yet!

Golden Dahl & Spinach

This makes a fantastic soup, but you could also easily turn it into a side or main dish by simmering for longer until you get a thicker consistency. The split peas do not need to be soaked beforehand.

Serves 4

1 tablespoon olive oil or butter
1 onion, peeled and finely chopped
2 garlic cloves, peeled and finely chopped
2cm fresh ginger, peeled and finely chopped
1 chilli, deseeded (optional) and finely chopped
350g yellow split peas, rinsed
1 teaspoon ground turmeric
1 teaspoon coriander
2 stock cubes
250g washed spinach
a handful of finely chopped fresh coriander
salt and freshly ground black pepper

Heat a pot on a medium-low heat and add the oil or butter. Fry the onion, garlic, ginger and chilli for 5–10 minutes until soft and fragrant.

Add the split peas, turmeric and ground coriander and give everything a stir.

Pour in 1.5 litres of boiling water, crumble in the stock cubes, and then bring the pot to the boil. Turn down the heat and simmer for 45–50 minutes.

Remove the pot from the heat and add the spinach, stirring until it has wilted. Finish with the chopped coriander and serve.

Roasted Pepper, Lentil & Thyme

This is always a firm favourite with our younger customers as it has got a great consistency and sweet flavour.

Serves 4

2 red peppers, deseeded and quartered
1 tablespoon olive oil or butter
1 onion, peeled and roughly chopped
2 garlic cloves, peeled and finely chopped
200g red lentils, rinsed well
a few sprigs fresh thyme, leaves only
2 stock cubes
salt and freshly ground black pepper

Preheat the oven to 190°C. Put your quartered peppers on a baking tray and roast for 20 minutes.

Meanwhile, put the oil or butter in a pot over a medium-low heat and fry the onion and garlic for 5–10 minutes until they are soft.

Take the peppers out of the oven and, if you like, remove their blackened skin – it's up to you. I never bother. Add them to the pan along with the lentils and thyme leaves and give everything a good stir.

Pour in 1.4 litres of boiling water, crumble in the stock cubes, and then bring it all to the boil. Turn down the heat and simmer for 15–20 minutes.

Blend the soup and season to taste.

Butternut Squash and Peanut Curry

Think satay flavours mixed with Indian spices and the ever flavourful butternut squash. Pumpkin or sweet potato could also be substituted in if you'd prefer. I like to garnish the soup with a few chopped salted peanuts for crunch.

Serves 4

1 tablespoon olive oil or butter
1 onion, finely sliced
2 garlic cloves, finely sliced
1 carrot, finely sliced
1 butternut squash, peeled, seeded and chopped
50g unsalted peanuts
1 teaspoon Madras curry powder
1 stock cube
salt and freshly ground black pepper

Put the oil or butter in a pot over a low heat, then add the onion, garlic and carrot. Fry for 5–10 minutes until they are soft.

Add the butternut squash, peanuts and curry powder into the pot, and give everything a stir.

Pour in 1.2 litres of boiling water and crumble in the stock cube, then turn up the heat and bring to the boil.

Turn down the heat and simmer for 15–20 minutes, then blend the soup to give it a really smooth texture. Season to taste.

Smoked Chipotle Chilli Bean

This soup is even more delicious garnished with a handful of tortilla chips and a dollop of sour cream or crème fraîche.

Serves 4

1 tablespoon olive oil or butter
1 onion, peeled and diced
2 garlic cloves, peeled and finely chopped
8 new potatoes, diced into 1–2cm cubes
5 tomatoes, quartered
1 dried chipotle chilli
1 teaspoon smoked paprika
1 × 400g tin mixed beans, drained
2 stock cubes
salt and freshly ground black pepper

Heat a pot on a medium heat and add the oil or butter. Fry the onion and garlic for 5–10 minutes until soft.

Add the potatoes, tomatoes, whole chipotle chilli, smoked paprika and drained beans and give it a good mix.

Pour in 1.2 litres of boiling water, crumble in the stock cubes, and then bring the pot to the boil. Lower the heat and simmer for 20 minutes.

Take out the whole chilli. If you like things hot, cut off the chilli stalk, then chop the rest of it up and stir it back into the soup. If not, just discard it. Season the soup and serve.

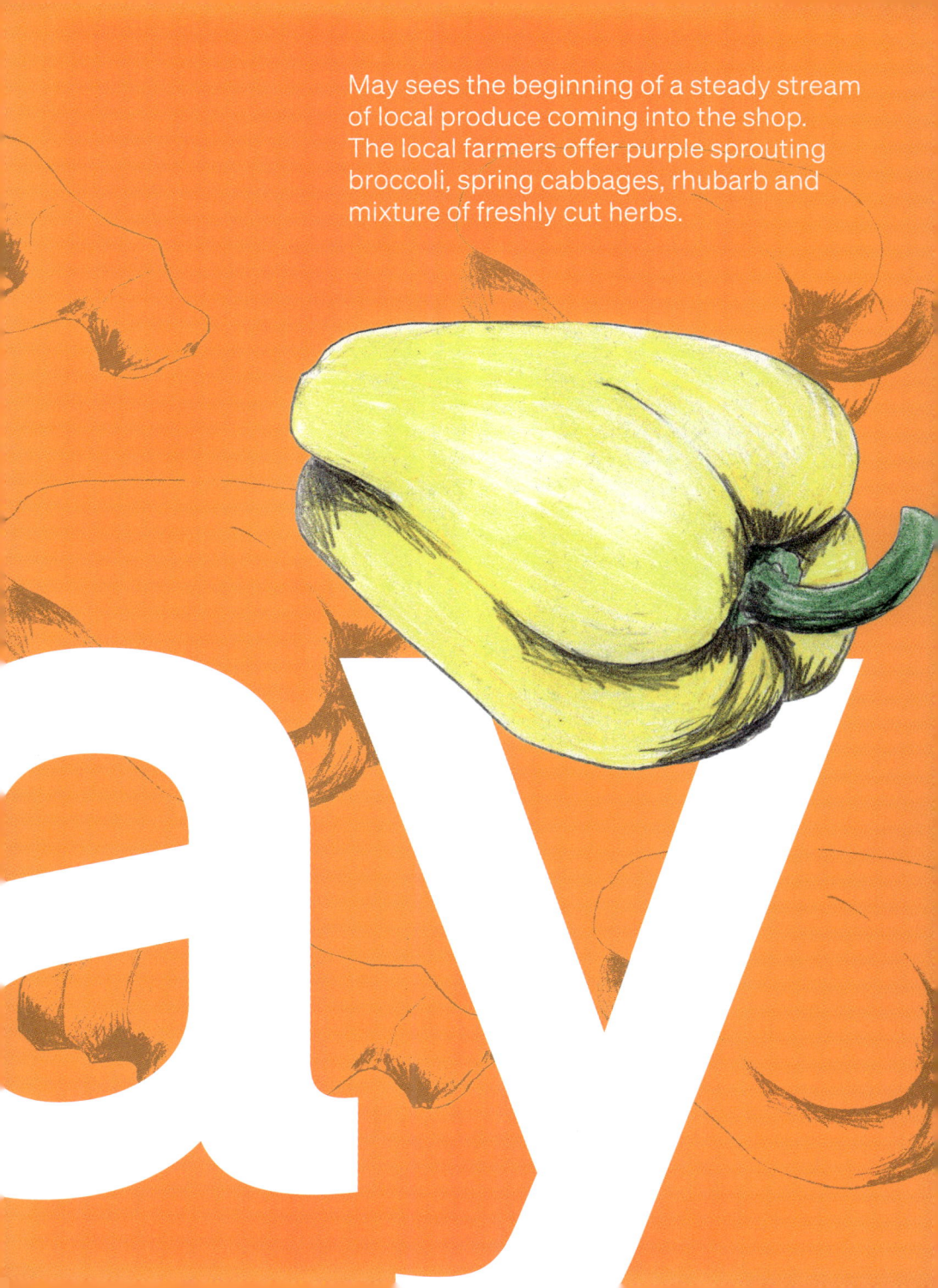
May sees the beginning of a steady stream of local produce coming into the shop. The local farmers offer purple sprouting broccoli, spring cabbages, rhubarb and mixture of freshly cut herbs.

Asian Noodle Broth

Use any kind of spring cabbage that's not very tightly packed for this one.

Serves 4

1 tablespoon sunflower oil
1 carrot, peeled and very finely chopped
thumb-sized piece fresh ginger, peeled and very finely chopped
2 garlic cloves, peeled and crushed
1 chilli, deseeded (optional) and finely chopped
¼ leafy cabbage, very finely shredded
2 stock cubes
2 dried noodle nests
1 spring onion, finely chopped

Heat the oil in a pot over a medium-low heat, and fry the carrot, ginger, garlic and chilli for 5–10 minutes until soft.

Stir in the cabbage, and then pour in 1.6 litres of boiling water. Crumble in the stock cubes, add the noodles and then bring it to the boil and simmer for 5 minutes or until the noodles are cooked.

Garnish the soup with the chopped spring onions, and feel free to add a couple of dashes of soy sauce or sesame oil to finish it off.

Creamy Mexican Tomato

A vegan, Mexican-inspired take on Cream of Tomato soup, with a silky, creamy texture from the cashews and the rich smoky spice of smoked chilli.

Serves 4

1 tablespoon olive oil or butter
1 onion, finely chopped
1 carrot, finely chopped
2 garlic cloves, finely chopped
750g medium tomatoes, diced
50g unsalted cashew nuts
1 dried Mexican chilli (chipotle, ancho or mulato)
1 stock cube

Put the oil or butter in a pot over a medium-low heat, then add the onion, carrot and garlic and fry gently for 5–10 minutes until they are soft.

Add the tomatoes, cashews and whole dried chilli and give it a good mix.

Pour in 1.2 litres of boiling water and crumble in the stock cube. Bring to the boil and then lower the heat and simmer for 20 minutes.

If you would like it spicy, chop up half the chilli and stir it back into the soup. If not, just discard it. Blend the soup for about 2 minutes to get a nice creamy consistency.

Italian White Bean & Cherry Tomato

If you can find some fresh oregano or have some in the garden, then pick the leaves from a couple of sprigs instead of using dried oregano.

Serves 4

- 1 tablespoon olive oil or butter
- 1 onion, peeled and finely chopped
- 1 carrot, peeled and finely chopped
- 1 courgette, finely chopped
- 2 garlic cloves, peeled and finely chopped
- 10 cherry tomatoes, halved
- 1 × 400g tin cannellini beans, drained
- 1 teaspoon dried oregano
- 2 stock cubes
- a sprig of fresh basil
- salt and freshly ground black pepper

Heat the oil or butter in a pot over a medium-low heat. Fry the onion, carrot, courgette and garlic for 5–10 minutes until they are soft.

Pop in the cherry tomatoes along with the beans and oregano and mix everything together.

Add a litre of boiling water and the crumbled stock cubes, and then bring everything to the boil. Turn down the heat and simmer for 15 minutes.

Season to taste and garnish with a couple of fresh basil leaves.

Cajun Black-Eyed Bean

I was making some gumbo one evening and thought – I could turn this into a soup. This is the easy version but if you can find any okra then a small handful wouldn't go amiss. This soup is really great garnished with a handful of tortilla chips to add some crunch.

Serves 4

1 tablespoon olive oil or butter
1 onion, peeled and diced into 1–2cm cubes
1 green pepper, deseeded and diced into 2cm cubes
2 celery sticks, finely sliced
2 garlic cloves, peeled and finely chopped
3 tomatoes, roughly chopped
1 × 400g tin black-eyed beans, drained
1 teaspoon smoked paprika
a pinch cayenne pepper
a pinch dried thyme
2 stock cubes
salt and freshly ground black pepper

Heat a pot on a medium-low heat and add the oil or butter. Fry the onions, green pepper, celery and garlic for 5–10 minutes until they soften.

Add the tomatoes to the pot along with the black-eyed beans and the spices and continue to cook for 5 minutes, stirring to stop anything sticking.

Pour in 1.2 litres of boiling water, crumble in the stock cubes, and then bring everything to the boil. Turn down the heat and simmer gently for 20–25 minutes.

Season to taste with salt and lots of freshly ground black pepper.

What a month for fresh produce! It's the start of the local berries, fresh peas, beans and new potatoes. Also the Spanish stone fruit season begins so grab as many peaches, nectarines and cherries as you can get your hands on... they're never better.

Pea & Mint

The classic summer soup – why try and change one of the best flavour matches in the world? If you can get a hold of apple mint then this gives the soup a different twist. You can use fresh podded peas, the same weight of frozen peas or make this in the winter with split peas. For the split pea option, use 350g split peas and add an extra 200ml of boiling water; then boil hard for 5 minutes and simmer for another 40.

Serves 4

1 tablespoon olive oil or butter
1 onion, peeled and diced
1 celery stick, diced
1 carrot, peeled and diced
2 garlic cloves, peeled and finely chopped
500g peas (podded weight)
a handful fresh mint, finely chopped (or a teaspoon of dried)
1 stock cube
salt and freshly ground black pepper

Heat the oil or butter in a pot over a medium-low heat, then add the onion, celery, carrot and garlic and fry for 5–10 minutes until soft.

Stir in the peas and mint, and then add a litre of boiling water and the crumbled stock cube. Bring everything to the boil, and then turn down the heat and simmer for 15 minutes.

Season to taste and blend until smooth.

Chorba Bissar

This is an everyday soup in North Africa and makes great use of fresh broad beans. Out of season you can make it with dried broad beans, but you will need to simmer the soup for more like 40 minutes.

Serves 4

- 1kg broad beans (unpodded weight)
- 1 tablespoon olive oil or butter
- 1 onion, peeled and roughly chopped
- 1 carrot, peeled and roughly chopped
- 2 garlic cloves, peeled and finely chopped
- 2 teaspoons paprika
- 1 teaspoon ground cumin
- 1 teaspoon garam masala
- 2 stock cubes
- salt and freshly ground black pepper

Pod the broad beans.

Heat a pot on a medium-low heat and add the oil or butter. Fry the onion, carrot and garlic for 5–10 minutes until soft.

Stir in the podded broad beans and spices and give everything a mix.

Add 1.2 litres of boiling water and the crumbled stock cubes, and then bring the pot to the boil. Reduce the heat and simmer for 20 minutes.

Blitz the soup until it is smooth and season well to taste.

Jamaican Curried Banana

Please trust us on this one – it's delicious! We like to serve it and let people guess what the ingredients are: they are so confused when you tell them it's banana soup. You can top each bowl with some banana chips if you want to give the game away. The Scotch bonnet chilli pepper is optional, but it gives a real Caribbean kick.

Serves 4

- 1 tablespoon olive oil or butter
- 1 onion, peeled and roughly chopped
- 2 garlic cloves, peeled and finely chopped
- 1 carrot, peeled and roughly chopped
- 1 sweet potato, peeled and roughly chopped
- 1½ teaspoons curry powder
- 2 bananas (preferably greener ones), peeled and roughly chopped
- 2 stock cubes
- 1 Scotch bonnet chilli pepper, whole (optional)
- salt and freshly ground black pepper

Heat a pot on a medium-low heat and add the oil or butter. Add the onion and garlic and fry for 5–10 minutes until soft.

Stir in the carrot, sweet potato and curry powder, giving everything a good mix, and then put in the chopped bananas.

Pour in 1.2 litres of boiling water along with the crumbled stock cubes and the whole Scotch bonnet chilli. Bring everything to the boil and then simmer for 15–20 minutes.

Remove the chilli pepper before blending everything together, and then season the soup well to taste.

Kinda Minestrone

This is our take on a minestrone, using orzo as the pasta as it doesn't swell so much when cooking. Feel free to change up the greens to whatever is in season.

Serves 4

1 tablespoon olive oil
1 onion, peeled and diced
1 carrot, peeled and diced
2 garlic cloves, peeled and finely chopped
1 celery stick, diced
2 baby new potatoes, diced
100g leafy cabbage or kale, very finely sliced
400g tin chopped tomatoes
2 fresh tomatoes, quartered
50g dried orzo
1 teaspoon dried oregano
2 stock cubes (added to 1.4 litres boiling water)
salt and freshly ground black pepper

Heat the oil in a pot on a medium heat. When it's hot, add the onion, carrot, garlic, celery and potatoes and cook, stirring, for 10 minutes until they soften. Turn the heat down a bit if they start to brown.

Add in the finely chopped cabbage or kale, tinned and fresh tomatoes, orzo and oregano and continue to cook for a further 5 minutes.

Add 1.4 litres of boiling water, then crumble in the stock cubes. Turn up the heat and bring to the boil.

Turn the heat down to low and simmer the soup for 20 minutes or until the potatoes are tender.

Season to taste.

This is a great month whether you're growing vegetables in the garden or shopping at your local greengrocer. Local brassicas like broccoli and cauliflower are in full flow, along with the new season baby carrots and beetroots. Also, if you're growing courgettes, then you should have a glut of them this month.

Charlene's Ruby Soup

A luxurious ruby-coloured soup, this uses two kinds of fresh herbs which work wonderfully with the sweet beetroot and carrots.

Serves 4

1 tablespoon olive oil or butter
1 onion, peeled and roughly chopped
2 garlic cloves, peeled and finely chopped
2 tennis ball-sized beetroot, peeled and diced into 2cm cubes
4 medium carrots, peeled and diced into 2cm cubes
thumb-sized piece fresh ginger, peeled and grated
a small handful fresh coriander, finely chopped including the stalks
a small handful fresh parsley, finely chopped including the stalks
2 stock cubes
salt and freshly ground black pepper

Heat a pot on a medium-low heat and add the oil or butter. Fry the onion and garlic for 5–10 minutes, until soft.

Add the beetroot, carrots, ginger and herbs and give everything a mix.

Pour 1.2 litres of boiling water into the pot and crumble in the stock cubes. Bring everything to the boil and then reduce the heat and simmer with the lid on for 25–30 minutes.

Blend the soup until it's smooth and season well to taste.

Plum Tomato, Orzo & Oregano

This is almost posh spaghetti hoops, and it doesn't take much longer than opening the tin and heating them up either. It uses a small pasta grain called orzo – if you can't find this then risotto rice or 50g of small pasta would work. If you can find some fresh oregano then pick the leaves off a few sprigs instead of using dried.

Serves 4

1 tablespoon olive oil or butter
1 onion, peeled and diced into 2cm cubes
2 garlic cloves, peeled and finely chopped
1 carrot, peeled and diced into 2cm cubes
1 stick celery, finely chopped
5 plum tomatoes, roughly chopped
100g orzo
1 teaspoon fresh oregano, chopped (or 1 teaspoon dried)
2 stock cubes
salt and freshly ground black pepper

Heat a pot on a medium heat and add the oil or butter. Fry the onion, garlic, carrot and celery for 5–10 minutes until they soften.

Add the roughly chopped tomatoes along with the orzo and oregano, and mix everything together.

Pour in 1.2 litres of boiling water, crumble in the stock cubes and bring to the boil. Then turn down the heat and simmer for 15 minutes.

Season to taste and feel free to garnish with some fresh basil on top.

Creamy Courgette, Cashew & Mixed Herb

This soup is light and incredibly smooth and creamy, and it can be enjoyed hot or chilled. It is also pretty cheap to make at this time of year. Any mixture of fresh herbs would work – I like basil, parsley and oregano.

Serves 4

1 tablespoon olive oil or butter
1 onion, peeled and roughly chopped
2 garlic cloves, peeled and finely chopped
1 large carrot, peeled and roughly chopped
2 or 3 courgettes, roughly chopped
50g unsalted cashew nuts
a handful fresh mixed herbs (or 1 teaspoon dried mixed herbs)
2 stock cubes
salt and freshly ground black pepper

Heat the oil or butter in a pot on a medium-low heat. Fry the onion and garlic for 5–10 minutes until they are soft but not coloured.

Add the carrots, courgettes, cashews and mixed herbs to the pot, mixing everything together.

Pour in 1.2 litres of boiling water, crumble in the stock cubes and bring to the boil. Reduce the heat and simmer for 20 minutes.

Blend the soup for at least 3 minutes for a really silky smooth finish and season to taste.

Broc-A-Leekie

This is a handy veggie soup for using up those wrinkly peppers or soft leeks at the end of the week.

Serves 4

1 tablespoon olive oil or butter
1 leek, washed and finely chopped
1 small red or green pepper, deseeded and roughly chopped
2 garlic cloves, peeled and finely chopped
1 head broccoli, roughly chopped (including the stalk)
1 medium potato, peeled and roughly chopped
2cm fresh ginger, peeled and grated
2 stock cubes
salt and freshly ground black pepper

Heat a pot on a medium-low heat and add the oil or butter. Add the leek, pepper and garlic and then fry for 5–10 minutes until they soften.

Mix in the broccoli, potato and grated ginger and continue to cook for 2 minutes.

Pour in 1.2 litres of boiling water, crumble in the stock cubes and bring to the boil. Turn down the heat and simmer for 25 minutes.

Blend the soup 'til smooth and season to taste.

It's probably my favourite month for seasonal produce: you still have the lovely peaches, nectarines and apricots but glimpses of Autumn are on the way with the beginning of the British plum season. We also get loads of great local produce in, including chillies, peppers and fennel.

just

Spiced Tomato Dahl

I took the dhal we make in the house and turned it into soup! It's delicious, with layers of flavour and texture – basically a big hug in a bowl.

Serves 4

1 tablespoon olive or sunflower oil
1 teaspoon coriander seeds
1 teaspoon cumin seeds
1 teaspoon turmeric
1 onion, peeled and diced
2 garlic cloves, finely chopped
1 chilli, finely chopped
500g fresh tomatoes, diced
1 small piece of ginger, peeled and grated
175g red lentils
1 stock cube
1 spring onion, finely chopped
salt and freshly ground black pepper

Heat the oil in a pot over a low heat and fry the coriander, cumin and turmeric until the seeds start to pop.

Add the onion, chilli and garlic to the pot and cook on a low heat for 10 minutes.

Add the tomatoes and ginger and cook for two minutes, and then add the lentils.

Pour in 1.2 litres of boiling water and crumble in the stock cube. Give everything a stir, turn up the heat and bring it to the boil.

Turn down the heat and simmer for 30 minutes, then season to taste with salt and freshly ground black pepper. Garnish with the finely chopped spring onion.

Carrot, Courgette & Chilli

This is one of our most popular soups; the courgettes make it silky smooth. Deseed the chilli if you don't like it too hot.

Serves 4

1 tablespoon olive oil or butter
1 onion, peeled and roughly chopped
2 garlic cloves, peeled and finely chopped
4 or 5 medium carrots, peeled and roughly chopped
2 courgettes, roughly chopped
1 chilli, finely chopped
2 stock cubes
salt and freshly ground black pepper

Heat a pot on a medium-low heat and add the oil or butter. Fry the onion and garlic for 5–10 minutes until soft.

Add the carrots, courgettes and chilli to the pot, mixing everything together.

Pour in 1.2 litres of boiling water and the crumbled stock cubes, turn up the heat and bring it to the boil. Reduce the heat and simmer for 20 minutes.

Blend the soup and season to taste. Add a little more sliced fresh chilli to the bowl if you'd like more heat.

Sweet Summer Lentil

A fun summer soup which can be altered by swapping fresh nectarines or peaches for the apricots.

Serves 4

1 tablespoon olive oil or butter
1 onion, peeled and roughly chopped
2 garlic cloves, peeled and finely chopped
1 teaspoon coriander seeds
1 teaspoon cumin seeds
3 plum tomatoes, roughly chopped
3 or 4 apricots, destoned and roughly chopped (or 8 dried apricots, roughly chopped)
175g red lentils, washed well
2 stock cubes
salt and freshly ground black pepper

Heat a pot on a medium-low heat and add a tablespoon of oil or butter. Fry the onion and garlic for 5–10 minutes until soft.

Meanwhile toast the spices in a dry frying pan for a few minutes until they start to release their smell. Stir them into the onions and garlic.

Add the roughly chopped tomatoes, apricots and lentils to the pot, and stir it all well.

Pour in 1.2 litres of boiling water, crumble in the stock cubes and bring to the boil. Reduce the heat and simmer for 20 minutes.

Season to taste and serve.

Roasted Pepper, Butterbean & Rosemary

You can give this a more Spanish flavour by adding a teaspoon of smoked paprika at the same time as the beans, peppers and rosemary.

Serves 4

2 red peppers, deseeded and quartered
1½ tablespoons olive oil
1 onion, peeled and roughly chopped
2 garlic cloves, peeled and finely chopped
1 or 2 carrots, peeled and roughly chopped
1 × 400g tin butterbeans, drained
1 rosemary sprig, leaves picked and finely chopped
2 stock cubes
salt and freshly ground black pepper

Preheat the oven to 190°C. Put the quartered red peppers on a baking tray, drizzle with half a tablespoon of olive oil and pop them into the oven for 20 minutes.

Meanwhile put a pot on a medium-low heat and add the remaining tablespoon of oil. Fry the onion, garlic and carrots for 5–10 minutes until they soften slightly.

Add the drained butterbeans and the roasted peppers to the pot – you can peel off the blackened skin of the peppers if you like, but I don't usually bother. Sprinkle over the rosemary and stir everything together.

Pour in 1.2 litres of boiling water, crumble in the stock cubes and bring to the boil. Turn down the heat and simmer for 20 minutes.

Blend the soup and season to taste.

People always come into the shop and tell us that it's soup time again – we make soup all year round but the great produce in the shop at this time of year must inspire the customers. We have Scottish sweetcorn, local squash and pumpkins. September is also the best month to get a wide variety of British apples and pears: look out for our favourite apple varieties Delbard Estevale, Early Windsor and Zonga.

Creamy Sweetcorn Chowder

This is a really good, thick soup that makes the most of fresh Scottish sweetcorn. Out of season you can use tinned sweetcorn and it will be nearly as good – just add it at the end of the cooking time and let it heat through.

Serves 4

1 tablespoon olive oil or butter
1 leek, washed and finely chopped
2 fresh sweetcorn cobs (or 1 x 340g tin, drained)
5 medium potatoes, peeled and diced into 2cm cubes
2 carrots, peeled and roughly chopped
2 stock cubes
a handful fresh parsley, very finely chopped
salt and freshly ground black pepper

Heat a pot on a medium-low heat and add the oil or butter. Fry the leek gently for 10 minutes.

Using a sharp knife, slice the sweetcorn kernels off the cobs. Add the fresh corn kernels, potatoes and carrots to the pot and give it a good stir.

Pour in 1.2 litres of boiling water, throw in the crumbled stock cubes and bring to the boil. Turn down the heat and simmer for 20 minutes.

If you're using tinned sweetcorn, drain it and stir it in now and heat through for a minute.

Blend the soup until smooth and creamy and then season to taste with salt and plenty of freshly ground black pepper.

Sprinkle some chopped parsley over each serving.

Moroccan Butternut Squash

The flavours in this soup all work really well together. If you like, the butternut squash can be replaced by sweet potato or pumpkin.

Serves 4

1 tablespoon olive oil or butter
1 onion, peeled and finely chopped
2cm fresh ginger, peeled and finely chopped
1 butternut squash, peeled, deseeded and roughly chopped
8 dried apricots, halved
1 teaspoon ground coriander
1 teaspoon ground cumin
2 stock cubes
salt and freshly ground black pepper

Heat a pot on a medium-low heat and add the oil or butter. Fry the onion and ginger for 5–10 minutes until soft.

Add the butternut squash, apricots, coriander and cumin to the pot, giving everything a stir.

Pour in 1.2 litres of boiling water, crumble in the stock cubes and bring to the boil. Turn down the heat and simmer for 15–20 minutes, until the squash is tender.

Blend the soup thoroughly to give it a really smooth texture and season to taste.

Creamy Cauliflower & Coconut

Probably the soup we get the most good feedback on – I always imagine it's because people don't expect much from it and are more than pleasantly surprised. A cracking soup to make for guests and let them guess what's in it. It's also good topped with some toasted coconut chips.

Serves 4

- 1 tablespoon olive oil or butter
- 1 onion, peeled and roughly chopped
- 2 garlic cloves, peeled and finely chopped
- 1 carrot, peeled and roughly chopped
- 1 cauliflower, cut into florets
- 2 stock cubes
- 1½ tablespoons creamed coconut
- salt and freshly ground black pepper

Heat a pot on a medium-low heat and add the oil or butter. Fry the onion, garlic, carrot and cauliflower for 10 minutes until soft but not coloured.

Give everything a stir, and add 1.2 litres of boiling water, the crumbled stock cubes and the creamed coconut. Bring it all to the boil, stirring so the creamed coconut dissolves.

Turn down the heat and simmer for 15–20 minutes.

Blend thoroughly until very smooth and creamy and season well to taste.

Creamy Woodland Mushroom

A vegan-friendly cream of mushroom soup with sweet leeks and woody thyme. All of these ingredients can grow wild in the woods, which made me think they'd work really well together in a soup.

Serves 4

- 1 tablespoon olive oil or butter
- 1 leek, washed and finely chopped
- 2 medium carrots, peeled and roughly chopped
- 2 garlic cloves, peeled and finely chopped
- 60g unsalted cashews
- 350g chestnut or field mushrooms, quartered
- 2 fresh thyme sprigs, leaves picked
- 2 stock cubes
- salt and freshly ground black pepper

Heat a pot on a medium-low heat and add the oil or butter. When it's hot, add the leek, carrot and garlic and fry for 5–10 minutes until they soften.

Put in the cashews, mushrooms and thyme leaves and give everything a stir.

Pour in a litre of boiling water, then crumble the stock cubes into the pot and bring to the boil. Turn down the heat and simmer for 15–20 minutes.

Blend the soup until smooth and season to taste with salt and freshly ground black pepper.

Thai Sweet Potato

It's the Makrut lime leaves that really make this soup sing, but if you don't have any you can use a stalk of lemongrass. Either way, feel free to garnish each bowl with some chopped fresh coriander.

Serves 4

- 1 tablespoon olive oil or butter
- 1 onion, peeled and roughly chopped
- 2 garlic cloves, peeled and finely chopped
- 1 large sweet potato, peeled and roughly chopped
- 1 chilli, deseeded (optional) and finely chopped
- 2cm fresh ginger, peeled and grated
- 1 or 2 Makrut lime leaves
- 2 stock cubes
- 1½ tablespoons creamed coconut
- salt and freshly ground black pepper

Heat a pot on a medium-low heat and add the oil or butter. Fry the onion and garlic for 5–10 minutes until soft.

Add the sweet potato, chilli, ginger and lime leaves and give everything a stir.

Pour in 1.2 litres of boiling water and then add the crumbled stock cubes and creamed coconut. Bring everything to the boil. Turn down the heat and simmer for 20 minutes.

Remove the lime leaf, season the soup and blend until smooth.

It's amazing how much of October revolves around the final day of the month and it always has a special place in our hearts because we first opened up on October 31st. Certainly the shop will be full of local pumpkins of all shapes, sizes and colours, and we also get the first of the new season Brussels sprouts and parsnips. We always wait until the first frost of the season so that the starch turns to sugar and makes them very sweet.

Lentil Soup

This is the first soup bag we ever sold, and it's still the most daunting. How can you tell people how to make lentil soup? We find that grating the vegetables gives a lovely texture to the soup and saves hacking at the turnip with a sharp knife. Feel free to add a bit of chopped bacon with the onion and celery, or why not add a teaspoon of dried chillies or cumin to spice it up a bit?

Serves 4

1 tablespoon olive oil or butter
1 onion, peeled and chopped
1 celery stick, finely chopped
3 carrots, peeled and grated
1 small piece of turnip (roughly 300–400g), peeled and grated
175g red lentils, rinsed
2 stock cubes
salt and freshly ground black pepper

Heat a pot on a medium-low heat and add the oil or butter. Fry the onion and celery for 5–10 minutes until they are soft.

Add the carrots, turnip and lentils and give everything a stir.

Pour in 1.2 litres of boiling water, crumble in the stock cubes and bring to the boil. Turn down the heat and simmer for 30 minutes.

Season to taste. Delicious.

Pumpkin & Lemongrass

If you can't find pumpkin then you could substitute any kind of squash.

Serves 4

1 tablespoon olive oil or butter
1 onion, peeled and diced
1 carrot, peeled and diced
1 teaspoon ground coriander
1 teaspoon turmeric
1 lemongrass stalk, snapped in two and bashed a few times
1kg pumpkin, peeled, deseeded and diced
2 stock cubes
1½ tablespoons creamed coconut

Heat a pot on a medium-low heat and add the oil or butter. Fry the onion, carrot, spices and lemongrass for 5–10 minutes until soft.

Stir in the pumpkin and continue to cook for a few minutes.

Pour in 1.2 litres of boiling water, and throw in the crumbled stock cubes and creamed coconut, stirring until the coconut dissolves. Bring to the boil, then turn down the heat and simmer for 20 minutes.

Remove the lemongrass and blend until smooth.

Parsnip & Apple

The garlic and rosemary-infused olive oil makes this soup really special, so even if you think it sounds pointless please give it a try! It'll make the world of difference and is a neat trick to add intensified flavours when cooking.

Serves 4

2 garlic cloves, peeled and finely chopped
2 sprigs rosemary, leaves picked off and finely chopped
2 tablespoons olive oil
1 onion, peeled and roughly chopped
750g parsnips, peeled and roughly chopped
1 apple, peeled, cored and roughly chopped
2 stock cubes
salt and freshly ground black pepper

Put the chopped garlic and rosemary into a small bowl with the olive oil and set aside for 10 minutes to infuse.

Heat a pot on medium-low heat and add the infused oil to the pot along with the onion, parsnips and apple and fry for 10 minutes.

Pour in 1.2 litres of boiling water, chuck in the crumbled stock cubes and bring to the boil.

Turn down the heat and simmer for 20 minutes.

Blend the soup until smooth and season well to taste.

October

Veggie Mulligatawny

You could add some boiled rice to this soup after it's been blended to bulk it up a bit – either way it's good.

Serves 4

1 tablespoon olive oil or butter
1 onion, peeled and diced
1 sweet potato, peeled and diced
1 carrot, peeled and roughly chopped
1 celery stick, finely chopped
1 apple, peeled, cored and roughly chopped
1 tomato, roughly chopped
1 tablespoon curry power
2 stock cubes
salt and freshly ground black pepper

Heat a pot on a medium-low heat and add the oil or butter. Fry the onion, sweet potato, carrot and celery on a low heat for 10 minutes.

Add the apple, tomato and curry powder to the pot, giving everything a stir.

Pour in 1.2 litres of boiling water and the crumbled stock cubes, and then bring to the boil.

Turn down the heat and simmer for 20 minutes.

Blend the soup and season to taste – lots of black pepper is nice here.

This is the start of the really cold weather and all our customers, as if by magic or some animal instinct, are looking to load up on hearty meals to keep them cosy. A great month to get hold of all the best root vegetables and maincrop potatoes – our favourites are Maris Piper, King Edward and Desiree.

mber

Spicy Noodle Broth

Try adding a couple of dashes of soy sauce and plenty of freshly ground black pepper to the finished soup.

Serves 4

1 tablespoon sunflower oil
1 carrot, peeled and very finely chopped
thumb-sized piece of fresh ginger, peeled and very finely chopped
2 garlic cloves, peeled and finely chopped
1 chilli, deseeded (optional) and finely chopped
a handful of mangetout or sugar snap peas
2 or 3 chestnut mushrooms, quartered
2 Makrut lime leaves
2 stock cubes
1 dried noodles nest
1 spring onion, sliced
freshly ground black pepper

Heat the sunflower oil in a pot over a medium-low heat. Fry the carrot, ginger, garlic and chilli for 5–10 minutes until soft and fragrant.

Add the mangetout or sugar snap peas, mushrooms and lime leaves.

Pour in 1.6 litres of boiling water, and then throw in the crumbled stock cubes and noodles. Bring everything to the boil and then reduce the heat and simmer for 5 minutes.

Scatter some sliced spring onions on each bowl season with plenty of black pepper and serve.

Smoked Chilli, Sweet Potato & Barley

The dried smoked chillies we use here have a wonderful flavour and aren't too hot. If you like you can take the chilli out at the end of cooking, discard the stalk, chop the flesh and add it back into the soup.

Serves 4

1 tablespoon olive oil or butter
1 onion, peeled and roughly chopped
1 celery stick, finely chopped
1 sweet potato, peeled and roughly chopped
1 teaspoon smoked paprika
100g pearl barley
1 smoked chilli (either ancho, mulato or chipotle)
2 stock cubes
salt and freshly ground black pepper

Heat the oil or butter in a pot on a medium-low heat. Fry the onion and celery for 5–10 minutes.

Add the sweet potato to the pot, along with the smoked paprika and barley.

Pour in 1.4 litres of boiling water, and add the crumbled stock cubes and the whole dried chilli. Bring everything to the boil. Turn down the heat and simmer for 20–30 minutes.

Season to taste and serve.

Carrot, Apricot & Ginger

Another of the steady favourites, this is one of those flavour combos that just work. We sometimes add in a squeeze of orange or a pinch of cinnamon to give it that mulled wine flavour.

Serves 4

1 tablespoon olive oil or butter
1 onion, peeled and roughly chopped
2 garlic cloves, peeled and finely chopped
750g carrots, peeled and roughly chopped
thumb-sized piece fresh ginger, peeled and finely chopped
6 dried apricots, roughly chopped
a pinch ground nutmeg
2 stock cubes
salt and freshly ground black pepper

Heat a pot on a medium-low heat and add the oil or butter. Fry the onion and garlic for 5–10 minutes until soft.

Stir in the carrot, ginger, apricots and nutmeg.

Pour in 1.2 litres of boiling water and the stock cubes, and then bring to the boil. Turn down the heat and simmer for 30 minutes.

Blend the soup for a smooth texture or leave as it is, and season to taste.

Butternut Squash, Coconut & Apple

The apple in this soup acts as a sweetener and can easily be replaced by using a pear, peach or apricot.

Serves 4

1 tablespoon olive oil or butter
1 onion, peeled and roughly chopped
1 carrot, peeled and roughly chopped
1 teaspoon garam masala
1 butternut squash, peeled, deseeded and diced
1 apple, peeled, cored and roughly chopped
2 stock cubes
1½ tablespoons creamed coconut
salt and freshly ground black pepper

Heat a pot on a medium-low heat and add the oil or butter. Fry the onion, carrot and garam masala for 5–10 minutes.

Add the squash and apple and continue to cook for 5 minutes.

Pour in 1.2 litres of boiling water, and add the stock cubes and the creamed coconut, stirring to make sure it dissolves. Bring to the boil, then turn down the heat and simmer for 20 minutes.

Blend the soup until completely smooth, and then season to taste.

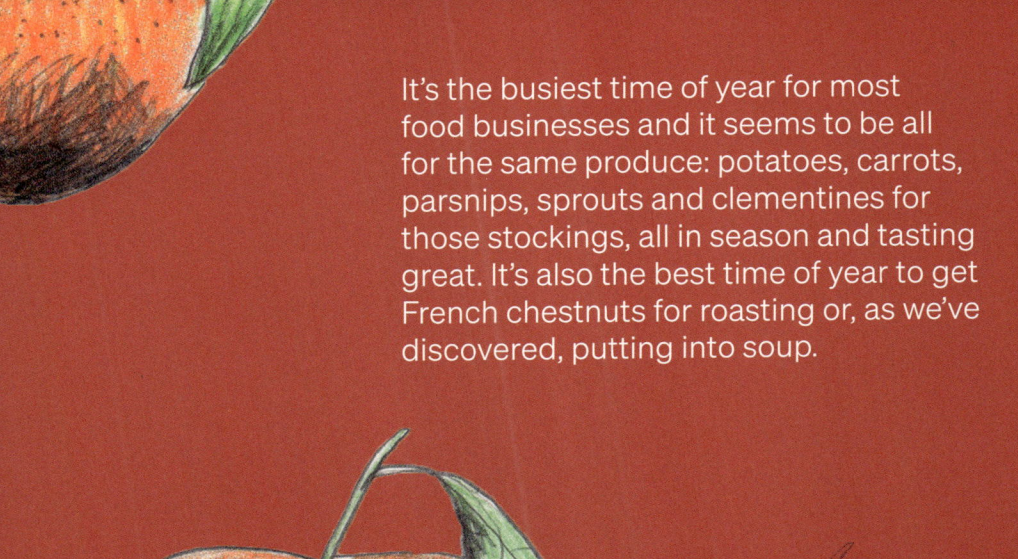

It's the busiest time of year for most food businesses and it seems to be all for the same produce: potatoes, carrots, parsnips, sprouts and clementines for those stockings, all in season and tasting great. It's also the best time of year to get French chestnuts for roasting or, as we've discovered, putting into soup.

Split Pea, Pear & Mixed Spice

This was a random concoction to try and shoehorn a pear into a soup. We are so glad that it worked because it is a truly stunning soup, excellent for impressing lunch guests, and it really tastes like Christmas.

Serves 4

- 1 tablespoon olive oil or butter
- 1 onion, peeled and roughly chopped
- 2 garlic cloves, peeled and finely chopped
- 1 pear, peeled and diced
- 2 carrots, peeled and roughly chopped
- 150g yellow split peas, rinsed
- 1 teaspoon mixed spice
- 2 stock cubes
- salt and freshly ground black pepper

Heat a pot on a medium-low heat and add the oil or butter. Fry the onion and garlic for 5–10 minutes until they soften slightly.

Add the pear and carrots to the pot along with the split peas and mixed spice. Give it all a stir.

Pour in 1.3 litres of boiling water, crumble in the stock cubes, then turn up the heat and bring to the boil. Boil hard for 5 minutes and then turn the heat to low and simmer for 30 minutes more.

Blend the soup and season to taste.

Tunisian Hot & Smoky Vegetable Soup

Harissa is the main flavour of this mixed vegetable soup. We only use a teaspoonful but the smoked chilli paste carries so much wonderful flavour that it can turn any ordinary dish into a masterpiece.

Serves 4

- 1 tablespoon olive oil or butter
- 1 onion, peeled and finely chopped
- 1 medium carrot, peeled and roughly chopped
- 1 medium courgette, roughly chopped
- 2 garlic cloves, peeled and finely chopped
- 1 medium sweet potato, peeled and roughly chopped
- 1 teaspoon harissa paste
- 300ml tomato passata
- 2 stock cubes
- salt and freshly ground black pepper

Heat a pot on a medium-low heat and add the oil or butter. When it's hot, add the onion, carrot, courgette and garlic and fry for 5–10 minutes until they soften slightly.

Put in the sweet potato and harissa and give everything a stir.

Pour in 900ml of boiling water and the passata, throw the crumbled stock cubes into the pot, and bring to the boil. Reduce the heat and simmer for 25 minutes.

Blend the soup until smooth and season to taste with salt and freshly ground black pepper.

Beetroot, Parsnip & Horseradish

This was inspired by a customer describing a soup which she'd had that was "pink, sweet and hot". We guessed it was something like beetroot mixed with parsnips, and we added the heat with horseradish root. A swirl of crème fraîche at the end will make this purple-coloured soup really attractive.

Serves 4

1 tablespoon olive oil or butter
1 onion, peeled and diced
1 garlic clove, peeled and finely chopped
300–400g raw beetroot, peeled and roughly chopped
3 medium parsnips, peeled and roughly chopped
thumb-sized piece fresh horseradish, grated
2 stock cubes
salt and freshly ground black pepper

Heat a pot on a medium-low heat and put in the oil or butter. Fry the onion and garlic for 5–10 minutes until nice and soft.

Add the beetroot and parsnips and give everything a mix. Stir about half of the grated horseradish into the pot.

Pour in 1.2 litres of boiling water, chuck in the crumbled stock cubes, and then bring to the boil. Reduce the heat and simmer with the lid on for 25–30 minutes.

Blend everything together and season well. Then have a taste and, if you feel like you can handle more horseradish, sprinkle some more straight into your bowl.

Chestnut, Carrot & Thyme

We tend to put this soup out at Christmas time as it works really well as a starter on the big day. It is luxurious enough but not overwhelmingly spicy or too filling. Try changing the flavours a bit by switching the carrots with parsnips and swapping the thyme with sage or rosemary.

Serves 4

1 tablespoon olive oil or butter
1 onion, peeled and roughly chopped
2 garlic cloves, peeled and finely chopped
1 stick celery, finely chopped
200g ready cooked chestnuts, roughly chopped
4 carrots, peeled and roughly chopped
a thyme sprig, leaves only
2 stock cubes
salt and freshly ground black pepper

Heat a pot on a medium-low heat and add the oil or butter. Fry the onion, garlic, celery, chestnuts and carrots for 10 minutes.

Sprinkle in the thyme leaves and continue to fry for another minute or so.

Add a litre of boiling water and the crumbled stock cubes, and then bring to the boil. Turn down the heat and simmer for 20 minutes.

Blend the soup until perfectly smooth and season to taste.

Sweet Chilli Lentil

A Thai-inspired twist on a traditional soup, changing the flavour dramatically by adding just a few ingredients. A great way to use up any leftover root vegetables after the big day.

Serves 4

1 tablespoon olive oil or butter
1 onion, peeled and diced into 1–2cm cubes
1 parsnip, peeled and grated
1 carrot, peeled and grated
2 garlic cloves, peeled and finely chopped
thumb-sized piece fresh ginger, peeled and grated
1 chilli, deseeded (optional) and finely chopped
175g red lentils, rinsed
1 or 2 Makrut lime leaves
2 stock cubes
1½ tablespoons creamed coconut

Heat a pot on a medium-low heat and add the oil or butter. Fry the onion, parsnip, carrot, garlic, ginger and chilli for 10 minutes, until everything is soft but not coloured.

Add the lentils and lime leaves and give it all a stir.

Pour in 1.2 litres of boiling water, and add the crumbled stock cubes and the creamed coconut, stirring to make sure it dissolves. Turn down the heat and simmer for 15–20 minutes.

Blend the soup 'til smooth or eat as it is – either way it's great!

Inc

lex

Index

A
almond:
    Golden Cauliflower & Almond 18
Alternative Scotch Broth 34
apple:
    Butternut Squash, Coconut & Apple 125
    Parsnip & Apple 113
    Veggie Mulligatawny 115
apricot:
    Carrot, Apricot & Ginger 123
    Sweet Summer Lentil 91
Asian Noodle Broth 57

B
banana:
    Jamaican Curried Banana 71
barley:
    Alternative Scotch Broth 34
    Smoked Chilli, Sweet Potato & Barley 120
bean:
    Cajun Black-Eyed Bean 62
    Italian White Bean & Cherry Tomato 60
    Roasted Pepper, Butterbean & Rosemary 92
    Smoked Chipotle Chilli Bean 53
    Smoky Sweet Potato & Butterbean 41
Beetroot, Parsnip & Horseradish 133
beetroot:
    Charlene's Ruby Soup 77
blood orange:
    Sweet Potato, Lentil & Blood Orange 28
broad bean:
    Chorba Bissar 68
Broc-a-Leekie 82
butterbean:
    Roasted Pepper, Butterbean & Rosemary 92
    Smokey Sweet Potato & Butterbean 41
Butternut Squash & Peanut Curry 50
Butternut Squash, Coconut & Apple 125
butternut squash:
    Moroccan Butternut Squash 99

C
Cajun Black-Eyed Bean 62
Carrot, Apricot & Ginger 123
Carrot, Courgette & Chilli 89
carrot:
    Alternative Scotch Broth 34
    Chestnut, Carrot & Thyme 134
    Persian Root & Fruit 16
    Charlene's Ruby Soup 77
cashew:
    Creamy Courgette, Cashew & Mixed Herb 80
cauliflower:
    Creamy Cauliflower & Coconut 100
    Golden Cauliflower & Almond 18
celeriac:
    Alternative Scotch Broth 34
    Charlene's Ruby Soup 73
Chestnut, Carrot & Thyme 134
Chilli Pepper Chickpea 36
chilli:
    Carrot, Courgette & Chilli 89
    Chilli Pepper Chickpea 36
    Smoked Chilli, Sweet Potato & Barley 120
    Smoked Chipotle Chilli Bean 53
    Sweet Chilli Lentil 136
Chorba Bissar 68
courgette:
    Carrot, Courgette & Chilli 89
    Creamy Courgette, Cashew & Mixed Herb 80
    Granny Smith Green 38
Creamy Cauliflower & Coconut 100
Creamy Courgette, Cashew & Mixed Herb 80
Creamy Mexican Tomato 59
Creamy Sweetcorn Chowder 97
Creamy Woodland Mushroom 103
Curried Banana 71
Curried Parsnip 31

D

dahl
    Golden Dahl & Spinach 46
    Spiced Tomato Dahl 87

G

Golden Cauliflower & Almond 18
Golden Dahl & Spinach 46
Granny Smith Green 38

I

Italian White Bean & Cherry Tomato 60

J

Jamaican Curried Banana 71

K

kale:
    Souper Noodle Broth 14
    Kinda Minestrone 73

L

Leek, Potato & Roasted Garlic 26
leek:
    Broc-A-Leekie 82
lemongrass:
    Pumpkin & Lemongrass 111
Lentil Soup 109
lentil:
    Golden Dahl & Spinach 46
    Roasted Pepper, Lentil & Thyme 48
    Spicy (or not) Tomato & Lentil 43
    Sweet Chilli Lentil 136
    Sweet Potato, Lentil & Blood Orange 28
    Sweet Summer Lentil 91

M

Mexican Tomato 59
Minestrone 73
Moroccan Butternut Squash 99
Mulligatawny 115
mushroom:
    Creamy Woodland Mushroom 103

N

noodle:
    Asian Noodle Broth 57
    Spicy Noodle Broth 119
    Souper Noodle Broth 14

O

orzo:
    Kinda Minestrone 73
    Plum Tomato, Orzo & Oregano 78

P

Parsnip & Apple 113
parsnip:
    Beetroot, Parsnip & Horseradish 133
    Curried Parsnip 31
    Persian Root & Fruit 16
Pea & Mint 66
peanut
    Butternut Squash & Peanut Curry 50
pear:
    Split Pea, Pear & Mixed Spice 129
pepper:
    Chilli Pepper Chickpea 36
    Roasted Pepper, Butterbean & Rosemary 92
    Roasted Pepper, Lentil & Thyme 48
Persian Root & Fruit 16
Plum Tomato, Orzo & Oregano 78
potato:
    Leek, Potato & Roasted Garlic 26
    Broc-A-Leekie 82
Pumpkin & Lemongrass 111

R

Rabbie Burns 21
roasted garlic
    Leek, Potato & Roasted Garlic 26
    Sweet Potato, Tomato & Roasted Garlic 12
Roasted Pepper, Butterbean & Rosemary 92
Roasted Pepper, Lentil & Thyme 48
Ruby Soup 77

S

Smoked Chilli, Sweet Potato & Barley 120
Smoked Chipotle Chilli Bean 53
Smoky Sweet Potato & Butterbean 41
Souper Noodle Broth 14
Spanish Split Pea 25
Spiced Tomato Dahl 87
Spicy Noodle Broth 119
Spicy (or not) Tomato & Lentil 43
spinach:
    Golden Dahl & Spinach 46
    Granny Smith Green 38
Split Pea, Pear & Mixed Spice 129
Sweet Chilli Lentil 136
Sweet Potato, Lentil & Blood Orange 28
sweet potato:
    Smoky Sweet Potato & Butterbean 41
    Smoked Chilli, Sweet Potato & Barley 120
    Thai Sweet Potato 105
    Veggie Mulligatawny 115
    Sweet Potato, Tomato & Roasted Garlic 12
    Sweet Summer Lentil 91
sweetcorn:
    Creamy Sweetcorn Chowder 97

T

Thai Sweet Potato 105
tomato:
    Creamy Mexican Tomato 59
    Italian White Bean & Cherry Tomato 60
    Plum Tomato, Orzo & Oregano 78
    Spiced Tomato Dahl 87
    Spicy (or not) Tomato & Lentil 43
    Sweet Potato, Tomato & Roasted Garlic 12
Tunisian Hot & Smoky Vegetable 131
turnip:
    Lentil Soup 109
    Persian Root & Fruit 16
    Rabbie Burns 21

V

Veggie Mulligatawny 115

Notes

Acknowledgements

I would like to thank the customers of Fraser's Fruit & Veg – without them the shop wouldn't exist and wouldn't be so much fun.

All members of the Fraser's Fruit & Veg team absolutely love opening our doors each morning and coming into work (even when it's -4°). Also, my publishers Emily and Nasim for maintaining focus and keeping me on the page (so to speak) whenever I procrastinate. I would like to thank Jen Collins who is a fantastic illustrator and friend; she truly doesn't know how good she is and drew lots of lovely pictures of fruits and vegetables for me many years ago and probably thought I'd never get round to using them. Thanks also to designer Andrew Forteath and photographer Clair Irwin for making this book look so good, and to Sandra Brown (www.sandrabrownceramics.com) for lending us her gorgeous bowls for the photoshoot. Thanks to Bethany Ferguson for her invaluable styling and prepping assistance at the shoot.

I would like to thank my family Paula, Ada and Hamish, who are my soup guinea pigs. Paula puts up with the mess I make in the kitchen and is forced to try all of the weird and wonderful soups that exist in my head. Her brutal honesty and hatred of woody herbs make soup creating both challenging and enjoyable.

To my Heinz tomato soup-loving children, stick in there, I promise that you will learn to love bananas in soup.

Finally I would like to thank my friends and family for their support in not only writing this book but helping me to achieve a life where you look forward to waking up every day and chatting to people about food. It is my passion; it's why I started the shop and there's nothing else I'd rather be doing every day.

Lastly I would like to thank my trusty wooden spoon. It's helped to make every single soup we'e ever put out and is still going strong twelve years later.